SAVAGISM
AND
CIVILIZATION.[1]

BY

HUBERT H. BANCROFT.

ISBN-13:
978-1727162547

ISBN-10:
1727162544

T HE terms savage and civilized, as
applied to races of men, are relative and not
absolute terms. At best these words mark
only-broad shifting stages in human
progress; the one near the point of departure,
the other farther on toward the unattainable
end. This progress is one and universal,
though of varying rapidity and extent; there
are degrees in savagism, and there are
degrees in civilization; indeed, though
placed in opposition, the one is but a degree
of the other. The Haidah, whom we call
savage, is as much superior to the Shoshone,
the lowest of Americans, as the Aztec is
superior to the Haidah, or the European to
the Aztec. Looking back some thousands of
ages, we of to-day are civilized; looking
forward through the same duration of time,
we are savages.

Nor is it, in the absence of fixed conditions,
and amid the many shades of difference
presented by the nations along our Western
sea-board, an easy matter to tell where even
comparative savagism ends and civilization
begins. In the common acceptation of these
terms, we may safely call the Central
Californians savage, and the Quichés of
Guatemala civilized; but between these two

extremes are hundreds of peoples, each of which presents some claim for both distinctions. Thus, if the domestication of ruminants, or some knowledge of arts and metals, constitutes civilization, then are the ingenious but half-torpid hyperboreans civilized, for the Esquimaux tame reindeer, and the Thlinkeets are skillful carvers and make use of copper; if the cultivation of the soil, the building of substantial houses of adobe, wood, and stone, with the manufacture of cloth and pottery, denote an exodus from savagism, then are the Pueblos of New Mexico no longer savages; yet in both these instances enough may be seen, either of stupidity or brutishness, to forbid our ranking them with the more advanced Aztecs, Mayas, and Quiches.

We know what savages are; how, like wild animals, they depend for food and raiment upon the spontaneous products of Nature, migrating with the beasts and birds and fishes, burrowing beneath the ground, hiding in caves, or throwing over themselves a shelter of bark, or skins, or branches, or boards, eating or starving as food is abundant or scarce; nevertheless, all of them have made some advancement from their original naked, helpless condition, and have acquired some aids in the procurement of their poor necessities. Primeval man, the only real point of departure, and hence the only true savage, nowhere exists on the globe to-day. Be the animal man ever so low—lower in skill and wisdom than the brute, less active in obtaining food, less ingenious in building his den—the first step out of his houseless, comfortless condition, the first fashioning of a tool, the first attempt ta cover nakedness and wall out the wind, if this endeavor springs from intellect and not from instinct, is the first step to civilization. Hence the modern savage is not the prehistoric or primitive man; nor is it among the barbarous nations of to-day that we must look for the rudest barbarism; if proof be wanting, there are the unground edges of the stone implements of Denmark, which denote an order of art lower than that indicated by any relic of the Stone age in America.

Often is the question asked. What is civilization? and the answer comes, The act of civilizing; the state of being civilized. What is the act of civilizing? To reclaim from a savage or barbarous state; to educate; to refine. What is a savage or barbarous state? A wild, uncultivated state; a state of Nature. Thus far the dictionaries. The term civilization, then, popularly implies both the transition from a natural to an artificial state, and the artificial condition attained. The derivation of the word civilization, from *civis,* citizen, *civitas,* city, and originally from *coetus,* union, seems to indicate that culture which in feudal times distinguished the occupants of cities from the ill-mannered boors of the country. The word savage, on the other hand, from *silva,* a wood, points to man primeval, *silvestres homines,* men of the forest, not necessarily ferocious or brutal, but children of Nature. From these simple beginnings both words have gradually acquired a broader significance, until by one is understood a state of comfort, intelligence, and refinement, and by the other humanity wild and beastly.

Guizot defines civilization as "an improved condition of man resulting from the establishment of social order in place of the individual independence and lawlessness of the savage or barbarous life;" Buckle as "the triumph of mind over external agents;" Virey as "the development more or less absolute of the moral and intellectual faculties of man united in society;" Burke as the exponent of two principles, "the spirit of a gentleman and the spirit of religion." "Whatever be the characteristics of a gentleman and the spirit of religion." "Whatever be the characteristics of what we

7

call savage life," says John Stuart Mill, "the contrary of these, or the qualities which society puts on as it throws off these, constitute civilization;" and, remarks Emerson, "a nation that has no clothing, no iron, no alphabet, no marriage, no arts of peace, no abstract thought, we call barbarous."

Men talk of civilization, and call it liberty, religion, government, morality. Now, liberty is no more a sign of civilization than tyranny; for the lowest savages are the least governed of all people. Civilized liberty, it is true, marks a more advanced stage than savage liberty, but between these two extremes of liberty there is a necessary age of tyranny, no less significant of an advance on primitive liberty than is constitutional liberty an advance on tyranny. Nor is religion civilization, except in so far as the form and machinery of sacerdotal rites and the abandonment of fetichism for monotheism become significant of intenser thought and expansion of intellect. No nation ever practised grosser immorality, or what we of the present day hold to be immorality, than Greece during the height of her intellectual refinement. Peace is no more civilization than war, virtue than vice, good than evil. All these are the incidents, not the essence, of civilization.

That which we commonly call civilization is not an adjunct or an acquirement of man; it is neither a creed nor a polity, neither science, nor philosophy, nor industry; it is rather the measure of progressional force implanted in man, the general fund of the nation's wealth, learning, and refinement, the storehouse of accumulated results, the essence of all best worth preserving from the distillations of good and the distillations of evil. It is a something between men, no less than a something within them: for neither an isolated man nor an association of brutes can by any possibility become civilized.

Further than this, civilization is not only the measure of aggregated human experiences, but it is a living working principle. It is a social transition; a moving forward rather than an end attained; a developing vitality rather than a fixed entity; it is the effort or aim at refinement rather than refinement itself; it is labor with a view to improvement, and not improvement consummated, although it may be and is the metre of such improvement. And this accords with latter-day teachings. Although in its infancy, and, moreover, unable to

9

explain things unexplainable, the science of evolution thus far has proved that the normal condition of the human race, as well as that of physical Nature, is progressional; that the plant in a congenial soil is not more sure to grow than is humanity with favorable surroundings certain to advance. Nay, more, we speak of the progress of civilization as of something that moves on of its own accord; we may, if we will, recognize in this onward movement the same principle of life manifest in Nature and in the individual man.

To things we do not understand we give names, with which, by frequent use, we become familiar, when we fancy that we know all about the things themselves. At the first glance, civilization appears to be a simple matter: to be well clad, well housed, and well fed; to be intelligent and cultured, are better than nakedness and ignorance; therefore it is a good thing a thins; that men do well to strive for—and that is all. But once attempt to go below this placid surface, and investigate the nature of progressional phenomena, and we find ourselves launched upon an eternity of ocean, and in pursuit of the same occult Cause, which has been sought alike by philosophic and barbaric of every age and nation; we find ourselves face to face with a great mystery, to which we stand in the same relation as to other great mysteries, such as the origin of things, the principle of life, the soul-nature. When such questions are answered as, What is attraction, heat, electricity; what instinct, intellect, soul? Why are plants forced to grow and molecules to conglomerate and go whirling in huge masses through space?— then we may know why society moves ever onward like a river in channels predetermined. At present, these phenomena we may understand in their action partially, in their essence not at all; we may mark effects, we may recognize the same principle under widely-different conditions, though we may not be able to discover what that principle is. Science tells us that these things are so; that certain combinations of certain elements are inevitably followed by certain results, but Science does not attempt to explain why they are so.

In every living thing there is an element of continuous growth; in every aggregation of living things there is an element of continuous improvement. In the first instance, a vital actuality appears; whence, no one can tell. As the organism matures, a new germ is formed, which, as the parent stock decays, takes its place, and becomes in

11

like manner the parent of a successor. Thus, even death is but the door to new forms of life. In the second instance, a body corporate appears no less a vital actuality than the first; a social organism in which, notwithstanding ceaseless births and deaths, there is a living principle. For, while individuals are born and die, families live; while families are born and die, species live; while species are born and die, organic being assumes new forms and features. Herein the all-pervading principle of life, while flitting, is nevertheless permanent, while transient is yet eternal. But, above and independent of perpetual birth and death is this element of continuous growth, which, like a spirit, walks abroad and mingles in the affairs of men. "All our progress," says Emerson, "is an unfolding, like the vegetable bud. You have first an instinct; then an opinion, then a knowledge, as the plant has root, bud, and fruit."

Under favorable conditions, and up to a certain point, stocks improve; by a law of natural selection the strongest and fittest survive, while the ill-favored and deformed perish; under conditions unfavorable to development, stocks remain stationary or deteriorate. Paradoxically, so far as we know, organs and organisms are no more perfect now than in the beginning; animal instincts are no keener, nor are their habitudes essentially changed. No one denies that stocks improve, for such improvement is perceptible and permanent; many deny that organisms improve, for, if there be improvement it is imperceptible, and has thus far escaped proof. But, however this may be, it is palpable that the mind, and not the body, is the instrument and object of the progressional impulse.

Man, in the duality of his nature, is brought under two distinct dominions: materially he is subject to the laws that govern matter, mentally to the laws that govern mind; physiologically, he is perfectly made and non-progressive; psychologically, he is embryonic and progressive. Between these internal and external forces, between moral and material activities there may be, in some instances, an apparent antagonism. The mind may be developed in excess and to the detriment of the body, and the body may be developed in excess and to the detriment of the mind.

The animal man is a bundle of organs, with instincts implanted that set them in motion; man, intellectually, is a bundle of sentiments, with an implanted soul that

13

keeps them effervescent; mankind in the mass, society—we see the fermentations, we mark the transitions; is there, then, a soul in aggregated humanity as there is in individual humanity?

The instincts of man's animality teach the organs to perform their functions as perfectly at the first as at the last; the instincts of man's intellectuality urge him on in an eternal race for something better, in which perfection is never attained nor attainable; in society, we see the constant growth, the higher and yet higher development; now, in this ever-onward movement are there instincts which originate and govern action in the body social as in the body individual? Is not society a bundle of organs, with an implanted soul of progress, which moves mankind along in a resistless predetermined march?

The strangest part of all is, that though wrought out by man as the instrument, and while acting in the capacity of a free agent, this spirit of progress is wholly independent of the will of man. Though in our individual actions we imagine ourselves directed only by our free-will, yet in the end it is most difficult to determine what is the result of free-will, and what of inexorable environment. While we think we are regulating our affairs, our affairs are regulating us. We plan out improvements, predetermine the best course, and follow it, sometimes; yet, for all that, the principle of social progress is not the man, is not in the man, forms no constituent of his physical or psychical individual being; it is the social atmosphere into which the man is born, into which he brings nothing, and from which he takes nothing. While a member of society he adds his quota to the general fund, and there leaves it; while acting as a free agent, he performs his part in working out this problem of social development, performs it unconsciously, willing or unwilling, he performs it, his baser passions being as powerful instruments of progress as his nobler; for avarice drives on intellect as effectually as benevolence, hate as love, and selfishness does infinitely more for the progress of mankind than philanthropy. Thus is humanity played upon by this principle of progress, and the music sometimes is wonderful: green fields, as if by magic, take the place of wild forests; magnificent cities rise out of the ground, the forces of Nature are brought under the dominion of man's intelligence, and senseless substance is endowed with speech and action.

As to the causes which originate progressional phenomena there are differences of opinion. One sees in the intellect the germ of an eternal unfolding; another recognizes in the soul-element the vital principle of progress, and attributes to religion all the benefits of enlightenment; one builds a theory on the groundwork of a fundamental and innate morality; another discovers in the forces of Nature the controlling influence upon man's destiny; while yet others, as we have seen, believe accumulative and inherent nervous force to be the media through which culture is transmitted. Some believe that moral causes create the physical; others, that physical causes create the moral.

Thus Mr. Buckle attempts to prove that man's development is wholly dependent upon his physical surroundings. Huxley points to a system of reflex actions—mind acting on matter, and matter on mind—as the possible culture-basis. Darwin advances the doctrine of an evolution from vivified matter as the principle of progressive development. In the transmutation of nerve-element from parents to children, Bagehot

16

sees "the continuous force which binds age to age, which enables each to begin with some improvement on the last, if the last did itself improve; which makes each civilization not a set of detached dots, but a line of color, surely enhancing shade by shade." Some see in human progress the ever-ruling hand of a Divine Providence, others the results of man's skill; with some it is free-will, with others necessity; some believe that intellectual development springs from better systems of government, others that wealth lies at the foundation of all culture; every philosopher recognizes some cause, invents some system, or brings human actions under the dominion of some species of law.

As in animals of the same genus or species, inhabiting widely-different localities, we see the results of common instincts, so in the evolutions of the human race, divided by time or space, we see the same general principles at work. So, too, it would seem, whether species are one or many, whether man is a perfectly created being or an evolution from a lower form, that all the human races of the globe are formed on one model and governed by the same laws. In the customs, languages, and myths, of ages and nations far removed from each other in

17

all social, moral, and mental characteristics,
innumerable and striking analogies exist.
Not only have all nations weapons, but
many who are separated from each other by
a hemisphere use the same weapon; not only
is belief universal, but many relate the same
myth; and to suppose the bow and arrow to
have had a common origin, or that all flood-
myths, and myths of a future life, are but
offshoots from Noachic and Biblical
narratives, is scarcely reasonable.

It is easier to tell what civilization is not, and
what it does not spring from, than what it is
and what its origin. To attribute its rise to
any of the principles, ethical, political, or
material, that come under the cognizance of
man, is fallacy, for it is as much an entity as
any other primeval principle; nor may we,
with Archbishop Whately, entertain the
doctrine that civilization never could have
arisen had not the Creator appeared upon
earth as the first instructor; for,
unfortunately for this hypothesis, the
aboriginals supposedly so taught, were
scarcely civilized at all, and compare
unfavorably with the other all-perfect works
of creation; so that this sort of reasoning like
innumerable other attempts of man to limit
the powers of Omnipotence, and narrow

them down to our weak understandings, is
little else than puerility.

Nor, as we have seen, is this act of civilizing
the effect of volition; nor, as will hereafter
more clearly appear, does it arise from an
inherent principle of good any more than
from an inherent principle of evil. The
ultimate result, though difficult of proof, we
take for granted to be good, but the agencies
employed for its consummation number
among them more of those we call evil than
of those we call good. The isolated
individual never, by any possibility, can
become civilized like the social man; he
cannot even speak, and without a flow of
words there can be no complete flow of
thought. Send him forth away from his
fellow-man to roam the forest with the wild
beasts, and he would be almost as wild and
beastlike as his companions; it is doubtful if
he would ever fashion a tool, but would not
rather with his claws alone procure his food,
and forever remain as he now is, the most
impotent of animals. The intellect, by which
means alone man rises above other animals,
never could work, because the intellect is
quickened only as it comes in contact with
intellect. The germ of development therein
implanted cannot unfold singly any more
than the organism can bear fruit singly. It is

a well-established fact that the mind without language cannot fully develop; it is likewise established that language is not inherent, that it springs up between men, not in them. Language, like civilization, belongs to society, and is in no wise a part or the property of the individual.

We may hold, then, *a priori,* that this progressional principle exists; that it exists not more in the man than around him; that it requires an atmosphere in which to live, as life in the body requires an atmosphere which is its vital breath, and that this atmosphere is generated only by the contact of man with man. Under analysis this social atmosphere appears to be composed of two opposing principles—good and evil—which, like attraction and repulsion, or positive and negative electricity, underlie all activities. One is as essential to progress as the other; either, in excess or disproportionately administered, like an excess of oxygen or of hydrogen in the air, becomes pernicious, engenders social disruptions and decay, which continue until the equilibrium is restored; yet all the while with the progress of humanity the good increases, while the evil diminishes. Every impulse incident to humanity is born of the union of these two opposing principles. For example, as I have said, and will attempt more fully to show further on, association is the first requisite of progress. But what is to bring about association? Naked nomads will not voluntarily yield up their freedom, quit their wanderings, hold conventions and pass resolutions concerning the greatest good to the greatest number; patriotism, love, benevolence, brotherly kindness, will not bring savage men together; extrinsic force must be employed, an iron hand must be laid upon them which will compel them to unite, else there can be no civilization; and to accomplish this first great good to man—to compel mankind to take the initial step toward the amelioration of their condition— it is ordained that an evil, or what to us of these latter times is surely an evil, come forward—and that evil is war.

Primeval man, in his social organization, is patriarchal, spreading out over vast domains in little bands or families, just large enough to be able successfully to cope with wild beasts. And in that state humanity would forever remain did not some terrible cause force these bands to confederate. War is an evil, originating in hateful passions and ending in dire misery; yet without war, without this evil, man would forever remain primitive. But something more is necessary.

War brings men together for a purpose, but it is insufficient to hold them together; for, when the cause which compacted them no longer exists, they speedily scatter, each going his own way. Then comes in superstition to the aid of progress. A successful leader is first feared as a man, then reverenced as a supernatural being, and finally himself, or his descendant, in the flesh or in tradition, is worshiped as a god. Then an unearthly fear comes upon mankind, and the ruler, perceiving his power, begins to tyrannize over his fellows. Both superstition and tyranny are evils; yet, without war, superstition, and tyranny, dire evils, civilization, which many deem the highest good, never by any possibility, as human nature is, could be. But more of the conditions of progress hereafter; what I wish to establish here is, that evil is no less a stimulant of development than good, and that in this principle of progress are manifest the same antagonism of forces apparent throughout physical Nature; the same oppugnant energies, attractive and repulsive, positive and negative, everywhere existing. It is impossible for two or more individuals to be brought into contact with each other, whether through causes or for purposes good or evil, without ultimate improvement to both. I say whether through causes or for purposes good or evil, for, to the all-pervading principle of evil, civilization is as much indebted as to the all-pervading principle of good. Indeed, the beneficial influences of this unwelcome element have never been generally recognized. Whatever be this principle of evil, whatever man would be without it, the fact is clearly evident that to it civilization, whatever that may be, owes its existence. "The whole tendency of political economy and philosophical history," says Lecky, "which reveal the physiology of society, is to show that the happiness and welfare of mankind are evolved much more from our selfish than what are termed our virtuous acts." No wonder that devil-worship obtains, in certain parts, when to his demon the savage finds himself indebted for skill not only to overthrow subordinate deities, but to cure diseases, to will an enemy to death, to minister to the welfare of departed friends, as well as to add materially to his earthly store of comforts. The world, such as it is, man finds himself destined for a time to inhabit. Within him and around him the involuntary occupant perceives two agencies at work; agencies apparently oppugnant, yet both tending to one end—improvement; and Night or Day, Love or Crime, leads all souls to the Good, as Emerson sings. The principle of evil acts as a perpetual stimulant, the principle of good as a reward of merit. United in their operation, there is a constant tendency toward a better condition, a higher state; apart, the result would be inaction. For, civilization being a progression and not a fixed condition, without incentives, that is without something to escape from and something to escape to, there could be no transition, and hence no civilization.

Had man been placed in the world perfected and sinless, obviously there would be no such thing as progress. The absence of evil implies perfect good, and perfect good perfect happiness. Were man sinless and yet capable of increasing in knowledge, the incentive would be wanting, for, if perfectly happy, why should he struggle to become happier? The advent of civilization is in the appearance of a want, and the first act of civilization springs from the attempt to supply the want. The man or nation that wants nothing remains inactive, and hence does not advance; so that it is not in what we have but in what we have not that civilization consists. These wants are forced upon us, implanted within us, inseparable from our being; they increase with an increasing supply, grow hungry from what they feed on; in quick succession, aspirations, emulations, and ambitions, spring up and chase each other, keeping the fire of discontent ever glowing, and the whole human race effervescent.

The tendency of civilizing force, like the tendency of mechanical force, is toward an equilibrium, toward a never-attainable rest. Obviously there can be no perfect equilibrium, no perfect rest, until all evil disappears, but in that event the end of progress would be attained, and humanity would be perfect and sinless.

Man at the outset is not what he may be, he is capable of improvement, or rather, of growth; but childlike, the savage does not care to improve, and consequently must be scourged into it. Advancement is the ultimate natural or normal state of man; humanity on this earth is destined some day to be relatively, if not absolutely, good and happy.

The healthy body has appetites, in the gratification of which lies its chiefest enjoyment; the healthy mind asserts more and more its independence. Increasing skill yields ever-increased delights, which encourage and reward our labor. This, up to a certain point; but with wealth and luxury comes relaxed energy. Without necessity there is no labor; without labor no advancement. Corporeal necessity first forces corporeal activity; then the intellect goes to work to contrive means whereby labor may be lessened and made more productive.

The discontent which arises from discomfort lies at the root of every movement; but, then, comfort is a relative term, and complete satisfaction is never attained. Indeed, as a rule, the more squalid and miserable the race, the more are they disposed to settle down and content themselves in their state of discomfort. What is discomfort to one is luxury to another; "the mark of rank in Nature is capacity for pain;" in following the intellectual life, the higher the culture the greater the discontent; the greater the acquisition, the more eagerly do men press forward toward some higher and greater imaginary good. We all know that blessings in excess become the direst curses; but few are conscious where the benefit of a blessing terminates and the curse begins, and fewer still of those who are able thus to discriminate have the moral strength to act upon that knowledge. As a good in excess is an evil, so evil as it enlarges outdoes itself and tends toward self-annihilation. If we but look about us, we must see that to burn up the world in order to rid it of gross evil—a dogma held by some—is unnecessary, for accumulative evils ever tend toward reaction. Excessive evils are soonest remedied; the equilibrium of the evil must be maintained, or the annihilation of the evil ensues.

Institutions and principles essentially good at one time are essentially evils at another time. The very aids and agencies of civilization become afterward the greatest drags upon progress. At one time it would seem that blind faith was essential to improvement, at another time skepticism— at one time order and morality, at another time lawlessness and rapine; for so it has ever been, and whether peace and smiling plenty, or fierce upheavals and dismemberments predominate, from every social spasm as well as fecund leisure, civilization shoots forward in its endless course. The very evils which are regarded as infamous by a higher culture were the necessary stepping-stones to that higher life. As we have seen, no nation ever did or can emerge from barbarism without first placing its neck under the yokes of despotism and superstition; therefore, despotism and superstition, now dire evils, were once essential benefits. No religion ever attained its full development except under persecution. Our present evils are constantly working out for humanity unforeseen good. All systems of wrongs and fanaticisms are but preparing us for and urging us on to a higher state.

If, then, civilization is a predestined, ineluctable, and eternal march away from things evil toward that which is good, it must be that throughout the world the principle of good is ever increasing and that of evil decreasing. And this is true. Not only does evil decrease, but the tendency is ever toward its disappearance. Gradually the confines of civilization broaden; the central principle of human progress attains greater intensity, and the mind assumes more and more its lordly power over matter.

The moment we attempt to search out the cause of any onward movement we at once encounter this principle of evil. The old-time aphorism that life is a perpetual struggle; the first maxim of social ethics, "The greatest happiness to the greatest number;" indeed, every thought and action of our lives points in the same direction. From what is it mankind is so eager to escape? With what do we wrestle? For what do we strive? We fly from that which gives pain to that which gives pleasure; we wrestle with agencies which bar our escape from a state of infelicity; we long for happiness.

There is another thought in this connection well worthy our attention. In orthodox and popular parlance, labor is a curse entailed on man by vindictive justice; yet, viewed as a civilizing agent, labor is man's greatest blessing. Throughout all Nature there is no such thing found as absolute inertness; and, as in matter, so with regard to our faculties, no sooner do they begin to rest than they begin to rot, and even in the rotting they can obtain no rest. One of the chief objects of labor is to get gain, and Dr. Johnson holds that "men are seldom more innocently employed than when they are making money."

Human experience teaches, that in the effort is greater pleasure than in the end attained; that labor is the normal condition of man; that in acquisition, that is progress, is the highest happiness; that passive enjoyment is inferior to the exhilaration of active attempt. Now imagine the absence from the world of this spirit of evil, and what would be the result? Total inaction. But, before inaction

can become more pleasurable than action,
man's nature must be changed. Not to say
that evil is a good thing, clearly there is a
goodness in things evil; and in as far as the
state of escaping from evil is more
pleasurable than the state of evil escaped
from, in so far is evil conducive to
happiness.

Another more plausible and partially correct
assertion is, that by the development of the
subjective part of our nature, objective
humanity becomes degenerated. The
intellectual cannot be wrought up to the
highest state of cultivation except at the
expense of the physical, nor the physical
fully developed without limiting the mental.
The efforts of the mind draw from the
energies of the body; the highest and
healthiest vigor of the body can only be
attained when the mind is at rest, or in a
state of careless activity. In answer to which
I should say that, beyond a certain point, it is
true; one would hardly train successfully for
a prize-fight and the tripos at the same time;
but that the non-intellectual savage, as a
race, is physically superior, capable of
enduring greater fatigue, or more skillful in
muscular exercise, than the civilized man, is
inconsistent with facts. Civilization has its

vices as well as its virtues, savagism has its advantages as well as its demerits.

The evils of savagism are not so great as we imagine; its pleasures more than we are apt to think. As we become more and more removed from evils, their magnitude enlarges; the fear of suffering increases as suffering is less experienced and witnessed. If savagism holds human life in light esteem, civilization makes death more hideous than it really is; if savagism is more cruel, it is less sensitive. Combatants accustomed to frequent encounter think lightly of wounds, and those whose life is oftenest imperilled think least of losing it. Indifference to pain is not necessarily the result of cruelty; it may arise as well from the most exalted sentiment as from the basest.

Civilization not only engenders new vices, but proves the destroyer of many virtues. Among the wealthier classes energy gives way to enjoyment, luxury saps the foundation of labor, progress becomes paralyzed, and, with now and then a noble exception, but few earnest workers in the paths of literature, science, or any of the departments which tend to the improvement of mankind, are to be found among the powerful and the affluent, while the middle

31

classes are absorbed in money-getting,
unconsciously thereby, it is true, working
toward the ends of civilization.

That civilization is expedient, that it is a
good, that it is better than savagism, we who
profess to be civilized entertain no doubt.
Those who believe otherwise must be ready
to deny that health is better than disease,
truth than superstition, intellectual power
than stupid ignorance; but whether the
miseries and vices of savagism, or those of
civilization, are the greater, is another
question. The tendency of civilization is, on
the whole, to purify the morals, to give equal
rights to man, to distribute more equally
among men the benefits of this world, to
meliorate wholesale misery and degradation,
offer a higher aim and the means of
accomplishing a nobler destiny, to increase
the power of the mind and give it dominion
over the forces of Nature, to place the
material in subservience to the mental, to
elevate the individual and regulate society.
True, it may be urged that this heaping up of
intellectual fruits tends toward monopoly,
toward making the rich richer and the poor
poorer, but I still hold that the benefits of
civilization are for the most part evenly
distributed; that wealth beyond one's
necessity is generally a curse to the

possessor greater than the extreme of poverty, and that the true blessings of culture and refinement, like air and sunshine, are free to all.

Civilization, it is said, multiplies wants, but then they are ennobling wants, better called aspirations, and many of these civilization satisfies.

If civilization breeds new vices, old ones are extinguished by it. Decency and decorum hide the hideousness of vice, drive it into dark corners, and thereby raise the tone of morals and weaken vice. Thus civilization promotes chastity, elevates woman, breaks down the barriers of hate and superstition between ancient nations and religions; individual energy, the influence of one over the many, becomes less and less felt, and the power of the people becomes stronger.

Civilization in itself cannot but be beneficial to man; that which makes society more refined, more intellectual, less bestial, more courteous; that which, cures physical and mental diseases, increases the comforts and luxury of life, purifies religions, makes juster governments, must surely be beneficial; it is the universal principle of evil which impregnates all human affairs, alloying even current coin, which raises the question. That there are evils attending civilization as all other benefits, none can deny, but civilization itself is no evil.